Early Intermediate to Intermediate

PIANO FOR BUSY TEENS
BOOK 1

12 Pieces with Study Guides to Maximize Limited Practice Time

Melody Bober • Gayle Kowalchyk • E. L. Lancaster

NAME_____

 Piano for Busy Teens

is designed for students who enjoy music and want to continue their study but have limited practice time. It includes music in varied styles—from original pieces in jazzy styles to favorite masterworks and arrangements of appealing themes from classical music. In addition, each book contains a Hanon study to further develop technical skills and a duet that can be played with a friend.

A *Study Guide* for each piece helps the student practice efficiently. It includes four sections:

 1-Minute FYI

Some background about the piece is provided *for your information*.

 5-Minute Warm-Up

These short examples will aid the student in learning the piece and can serve as a practice warm-up.

 15-Minute Practice Plan

This plan includes suggestions for dividing the piece into practice sections that will foster learning. The sections are labeled on each piece of music. Additional space is provided for notes or assignments by the teacher.

 5-Minute Finishing Touches

These ideas will make performances more interesting and exciting.

Alfred

Copyright © MMIX by Alfred Music Publishing Co., Inc.
All rights reserved. Printed in USA.
ISBN-10: 0-7390-6121-6
ISBN-13: 978-0-7390-6121-3

To the Teen

If you love music and piano lessons but don't have much time to practice, this book is for you. Here are some suggestions to make your study more successful.

✔ To make the most progress, spend a little time each day practicing—even if it is only 15 minutes.

✔ For each piece, practice sections in the following ways:

1. Tapping the rhythm hands together on your lap

2. Playing hands separately, with special attention to fingering, articulation and phrasing

3. Playing hands together, slowly

✔ Practice early in the day, before school or immediately when you come home.

✔ Work only on pieces that *really* appeal to you.

✔ Study only one or two pieces at a time and focus on small sections. Avoid playing the entire piece during initial practice sessions.

✔ Remember not to judge your success in piano study by comparing yourself to others. You are successful if you love music and enjoy playing the piano, regardless of how difficult your pieces are or how many pieces you learn each year.

To the Teacher

If you have students who love music and piano lessons, but have minimal practice time, this book is for them. Here are some suggestions to make their study more successful.

✔ Remember that teens are very busy with homework, extracurricular activities and sometimes work. Be flexible with students—realize music is important to them, but that they have limited practice time. Make assignments small and attainable.

✔ When students come to a lesson without practicing, avoid spending the *entire* time as a practice lesson. Devote time to listening to music and to music theory. Use the music that they are studying to teach music history and appreciation.

✔ Allow students to practice only one piece if that is what they have time to do. Let them choose the style of music to study.

✔ Adjust your expectations for study. All students do not have to participate in auditions, contests or recitals.

✔ Help students figure out their highest practice priority for the next week at the end of each lesson.

✔ Change repertoire before a piece is "perfected" if it increases musical knowledge and motivation.

✔ Remember that the most successful teacher is the one who instills the love of music into every student.

Contents

	STUDY GUIDE	MUSIC

4

StudyStudy
Guide

Fast Track Boogie

Melody Bober
(pages 6–7)

1-Minute FYI

- *Boogie* refers to "boogie-woogie" style, a form of piano blues that began in the early part of the 20th century.

- In boogie, a blues chord progression is usually supported by a repetitive and percussive left-hand bass pattern. See the bass pattern in measures 12–17 of *Fast Track Boogie*.

- Boogie was first used as the piano accompaniment for lively dances.

5-Minute Warm-Up

These exercises will help you with fingering changes.
Play each example 3 times a day.

1.

2.

3.

4.

5.

15-Minute Practice Plan

Divide *Fast Track Boogie* into three sections for practice.

Week 1:	Section 1 (measures 1–11)

Week 2:	Section 3 (measures 20–31)
✔ *Notice that Section 3 is similar to Section 1.*	

Week 3:	Section 2 (measures 12–19)

Week 4:	Practice the entire piece.
✔ *Work to gradually increase the speed of the piece.*	

⭐ 5-Minute Finishing Touches

- ✔ Perform *Fast Track Boogie* with energy and drive, always playing the eighth notes evenly.

- ✔ Measure 27 should sound like an echo of measure 26.

Study Guide

Study Guide: pages 4–5

Fast Track Boogie

Melody Bober

Study Guide

Rage Over a Lost Penny

Ludwig van Beethoven, arr. Melody Bober
(pages 10–11)

❓ 1-Minute FYI

✔ *Rage Over a Lost Penny* is an arrangement of the theme from Beethoven's *Rondo a capriccio* for piano.

✔ The work was first published in 1828 by the publisher and composer, Anton Diabelli. The manuscript was lost for many years and then found again in 1949 in the United States.

✔ In the original piece, the two-part theme is changed each time that it returns.

🦴 5-Minute Warm-Up

These exercises will help you with fingering changes.
Play each example 3 times a day.

1.

2.

3.

15-Minute Practice Plan

Divide *Rage Over a Lost Penny* into three sections for practice.

Study Guide

Week 1:	Section 1 (measures 1–10)
✔ *Focus on playing the RH louder than the LH.*	

Week 2:	Section 3 (measures 19–26)
✔ *Notice the slight differences between Section 1 and Section 3.*	
✔ *Focus on playing the RH louder than the LH.*	

Week 3:	Section 2 (measures 11–18)
✔ *Focus on playing the LH louder than the RH.*	

Week 4:	Practice the entire piece.

5-Minute Finishing Touches

- ✔ Even though the tempo is *vivace* (lively), make sure that it is not too fast to be comfortable during performance.
- ✔ Play all *staccato* notes crisply and with energy.
- ✔ Always bring out the hand that plays the melody.

Rage Over a Lost Penny

Ludwig van Beethoven (1770–1827)
Op. 129
arr. Melody Bober

Section 1

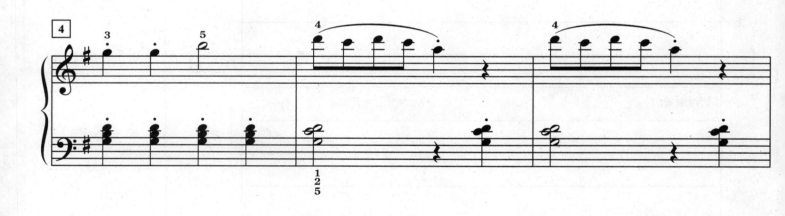

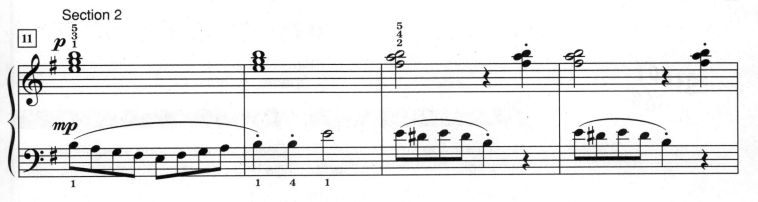

Section 2

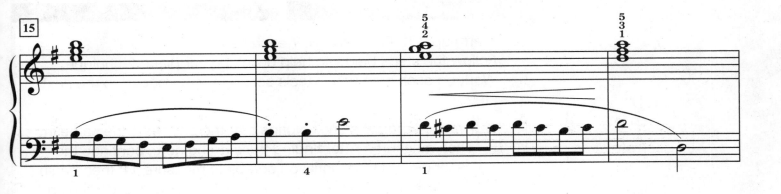

Section 3

Study Guide

Exercise No. 1

Charles-Louis Hanon
(pages 14–15)

❓ 1-Minute FYI

✓ This is the first exercise from Charles-Louis Hanon's technique book, *The Virtuoso Pianist*. This book contains 60 total exercises.

✓ Since its publication in 1873, pianists throughout the world have used these exercises to develop technical skills.

🎵 5-Minute Warm-Up

Warm up with *Exercise No. 1* each day.
Follow the steps below to help develop your piano technique.
Work on each step until it feels secure; then proceed to the next step.

1. Practice the LH alone. Notice that the pattern is the same in each measure. After finding the starting note, continue the ascending pattern until you complete measure 14; then begin the descending pattern in measure 15 until you reach the end. After you learn the pattern, it is not necessary to read every measure.

2. Practice the RH alone.

3. Practice hands together, slowly. Gradually increase the tempo, always listening for an even sound.

4. Practice hands together playing each note staccato.

5. Practice with a crescendo and diminuendo in each measure.

6. Practice with the following dotted rhythm in each measure.

etc.

7. Practice with the following triplet rhythm in each measure.

etc.

8. Transpose to G Major.

etc.

9. Transpose to D Major.

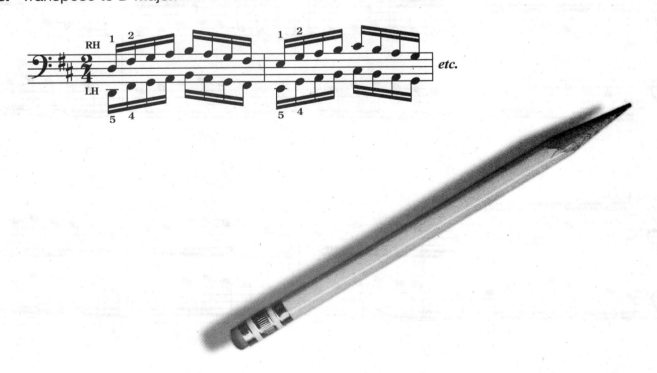

etc.

Study Guide: pages 12–13

Exercise No. 1
(from *The Virtuoso Pianist*)

Charles-Louis Hanon
(1819–1900)

15 Descending

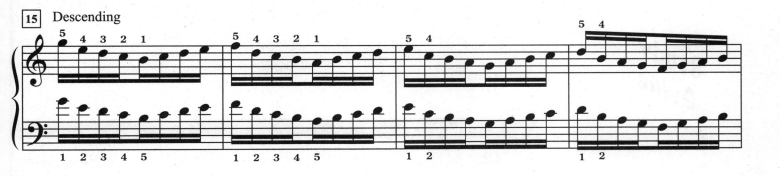

19

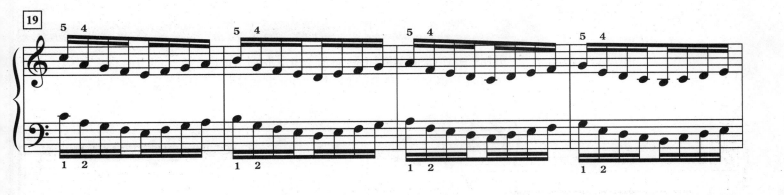

23

27

On a Mission

Melody Bober
(pages 17–19)

1-Minute FYI

- *On a Mission* is a jazz-style piece that is to be performed with a sense of urgency.

- The introduction establishes a two-measure descending bass line that predominates throughout the piece.

5-Minute Warm-Up

This exercise will help you get a feel for the key of the piece (A minor) as well as help with coordination. Play it 3 times a day.

15-Minute Practice Plan

Divide *On a Mission* into three sections for practice.

Week 1:	Section 1 (measures 1–20)
Week 2:	Section 3 (measures 28–46)
✔ *Notice that Section 3 is similar to Section 1. Compare the two sections and determine how they are different.*	
Week 3:	Section 2 (measures 20–28)
Week 4:	Practice the entire piece.
✔ *Warm up with the scales found in measures 7–8, 11–12, 19–20, 31–32, 35–36 and 43–45.*	

Study Guide

5-Minute Finishing Touches

✔ Play the eighth notes with a long–short rhythm pattern known as *swing style.*

✔ Play the LH a little softer than the RH.

✔ Follow the *crescendo* and *diminuendo* signs to give shape to the scale lines.

On a Mission

Section 1

Melody Bober

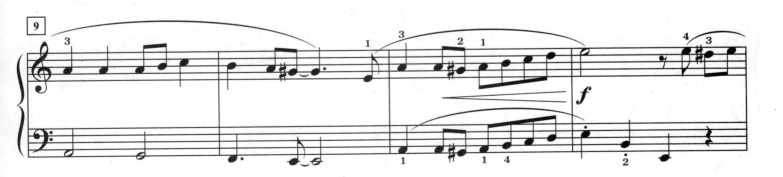

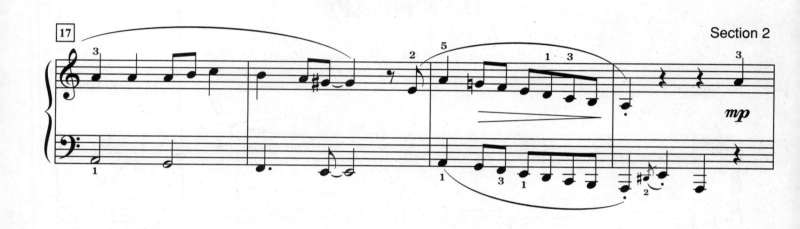

Section 2

LH quarter notes detached

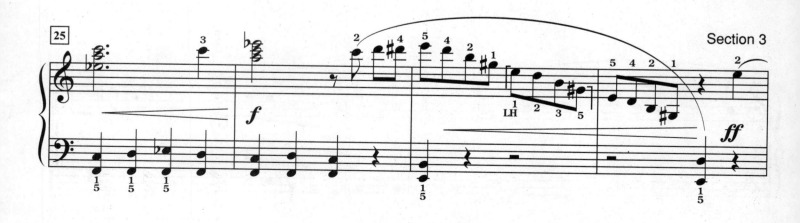

Section 3

Study Guide

Sonatina in C Major
(First Movement)

Frank Lynes
(pages 22–23)

❓ 1-Minute FYI

- A *sonatina* is a short *sonata* (a piece to be played on a musical instrument—not sung).

- This is the first movement of a three-movement *sonatina*.

- This movement has three sections and a coda:

  1. *Exposition*—two themes are stated.

  2. *Development*—the second theme is altered.

  3. *Recapitulation*—the two themes are restated.

  4. *Coda*—The ending section uses a C major scale in the RH.

5-Minute Warm-Up

These exercises will help you learn the broken chords and scales in the RH melody. Play each example 3 times a day.

1.

2.

3.

15-Minute Practice Plan

Study Guide

Practice each section of *Sonatina in C Major.*

Week 1:	Exposition (measures 1–14)
✔ Notice that the RH of measures 9–14 begins on a different note, but the pattern in each measure is similar. These similar patterns are called a sequence.	

Week 2:	Recapitulation (measures 19–32)
✔ Notice that the recapitulation is similar to the exposition. Compare the two sections and determine how they are different.	

Week 3:	Development (measures 15–18)
✔ The RH of measures 15–17 creates a sequence.	

Week 4:	Coda (measures 33–40)
✔ When playing hands together, first block (play at the same time) all 3 notes of the LH chord in each measure.	

 5-Minute Finishing Touches

- ✔ Play the LH a little softer than the RH.
- ✔ In the Coda, play the ascending RH scales with a small *crescendo* and the descending RH scales with a small *diminuendo.*
- ✔ Listen for a steady tempo throughout.

Sonatina in C Major
(First Movement)

Frank Lynes (1858–1913)
Op. 39, No. 1

Midnight Ride

Melody Bober
(pages 26–27)

1-Minute FYI

- *Midnight Ride* is a "showstopper" to highlight the performer's skill in executing RH runs and hand-over-hand patterns.

- The groups of three eighth notes in *Midnight Ride* give the piece energy and excitement.

5-Minute Warm-Up

These exercises will help you with the chromatic scale and cross-overs. Play each example 3 times a day.

1.

2.

two octaves lower on repeat

3.

4.

two octaves higher on repeat

15-Minute Plan

Divide *Midnight Ride* into three sections for practice.

Week 1:	Section 1 (measures 1–9)

Week 2:	Section 3 (measures 18–24)

✔ *Notice that Section 3 is similar to Section 1. Compare the two sections and determine how they are different.*

Week 3:	Section 2 (measures 10–17)

✔ *Bring out the LH in measures 10–11 and 14–15.*

Week 4:	Section 4 (measures 25–30)

✔ *Also, practice the entire piece by section. Work to gradually increase the speed of each section.*

5-Minute Finishing Touches

- ✔ Play all eighth notes evenly, without rushing.
- ✔ When eighth notes move from hand-to-hand, make them sound like one continuous line without breaks.
- ✔ As you perform, feel four strong beats in each measure.

Study Guide

Study Guide: pages 24–25

Midnight Ride

Melody Bober

Musette in D Major

Johann Sebastian Bach
(pages 30–31)

1-Minute FYI

✓ A *musette* is a small bagpipe that was popular in France in the 17th century and early part of the 18th century. This dance-like piece imitates the sound of a bagpipe.

✓ The left hand of this musette has octave figures that suggest a drone bass (repeated figures).

✓ This musette is from the *Notebook for Anna Magdalena*, a book of music that Johann Sebastian Bach compiled for his second wife.

5-Minute Warm-Up

This exercise will help you get a feel for the key of the piece (D major) as well as help with coordination. Play it 3 times a day.

These exercises will help you with jumps in both hands.
Play each example 3 times a day.

15-Minute Practice Plan

Divide *Musette* into four sections for practice.

Week 1:	Section 1 (measures 1–8)
	Section 4 (measures 21–28)

✔ *Notice that these sections are exactly the same.*

Week 2:	Section 3 (measures 13–20)

✔ *This is probably the most difficult section and may require*

extra practice to coordinate the two hands.

Week 3:	Section 2 (measures 9–12)

Week 4:	Practice the entire piece.

✔ *Spend extra time working on Section 3 (measures 13–20)*

before playing the entire piece.

 5-Minute Finishing Touches

✔ Play the LH octave figures softer than the RH melody.

✔ Observe the *moderato* tempo marking and avoid playing *Musette* too fast. This moderate tempo will aid with making the jumps in both hands.

Study Guide

Musette in D Major
(from the *Notebook for Anna Magdalena*)

Johann Sebastian Bach
(1685–1750)

31

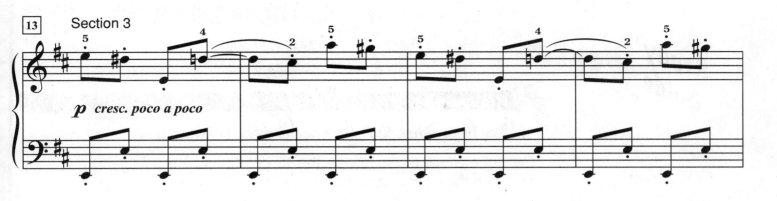

Section 3

Section 4

Study Guide

Love Those Blues

Melody Bober
(pages 33–35)

1-Minute FYI

- ✔ The *blues* developed from African-American folk music in the 20th century.

- ✔ *Love Those Blues* follows the 12-bar blues harmonic pattern. (See the warm-up below.)

- ✔ Blues is often associated with jazz, but it evolved as a separate form that exerted great influence on American popular music in the last half of the 20th century.

5-Minute Warm-Up

This exercise will help you learn the left hand of the piece as well as the 12-bar blues form. Play it 3 times a day.

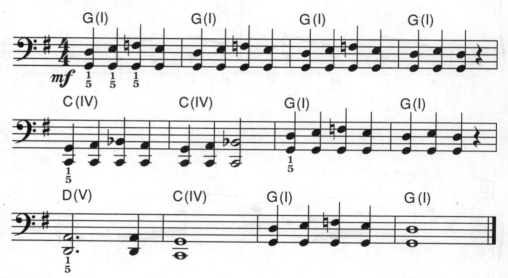

15-Minute Practice Plan

Divide *Love Those Blues* into three sections for practice.

Week 1:	Section 1 (measures 1–12)
Week 2:	Section 3 (measures 24–46)
✔ *Notice the similarities between Section 1 and Section 3.*	
Week 3:	Section 2 (measures 13–24)
Week 4:	Practice the entire piece.

5-Minute Finishing Touches

 Study Guide

- ✔ Play the eighth notes with a long–short rhythm pattern known as *swing style.*

- ✔ Play the LH a little softer than the RH.

- ✔ Perform the piece slowly with lots of feeling.

Love Those Blues

Melody Bober

LH quarter notes detached

13 Section 2

17

21 Section 3

25

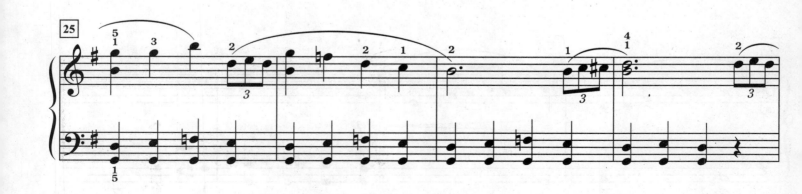

Arabesque

Johann Burgmüller
(pages 38–39)

1-Minute FYI

- *Arabesque* is a term borrowed from art. It is used to describe repeating ornamental geometric patterns.

- When applied to music, the word *arabesque* suggests ornamental figures. The ornamental figures in the Burgmüller *Arabesque* are the sixteenth notes.

- In addition to Burgmüller, Robert Schumann and Claude Debussy also composed *arabesques* for piano.

5-Minute Warm-Up

These exercises will help you with the chord changes and moves in the left hand. Play each example 3 times a day.

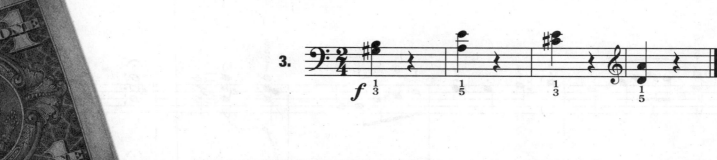

15-Minute Practice Plan

Divide *Arabesque* into six sections for practice.

Week 1:	Section 1 (measures 1–6)
	Section 4 (measures 20–23)
	Section 6 (measures 28–33)
Week 2:	Section 2 (measures 7–11)
	Section 5 (measures 24–27)
Week 3:	Section 3 (measures 12–19)
Week 4:	Measures 18–19
✔ *These measures can be tricky to coordinate. Practice hands together very slowly stopping on each eighth note to confirm that both notes and fingerings are correct.*	

5-Minute Finishing Touches

✔ In sections 1, 4 and 6, bring out the sixteenth notes above the notes in the other hand.

✔ Play all sixteenth notes evenly.

✔ Lift the hands for rests.

Study Guide: pages 36–37

Arabesque

Johann Burgmüller (1806–1874)
Op. 100, No. 2

Section 1
Allegro scherzando

Section 2

Section 3

dim. e poco rit.

Section 4

a tempo

Section 5

Section 6

p dolce

f risoluto

Emerald Fountain

Melody Bober
(pages 41–43)

 1-Minute FYI

- ✔ *Emerald Fountain* evokes a flowing style similar to a contemporary popular ballad without words.

- ✔ The lyrical, singing LH begins with a descending chromatic scale.

 5-Minute Warm-Up

These exercises will help you develop freedom to move around the keyboard. Play each example 3 times a day.

 15-Minute Practice Plan

Divide *Emerald Fountain* into four sections for practice.

Week 1:	Section 1 (measures 1–16)
Week 2:	Section 3 (measures 32–47)
✔ *Notice the similarities between Section 1 and Section 3.*	
Week 3:	Section 2 (measures 16–31)
Week 4:	Section 4 (measures 47–56)

5-Minute Finishing Touches

✔ Play the *rit.* and *poco rit.* at the end of sections with freedom.

✔ Listen for clear pedal changes.

Emerald Fountain

Section 1

Delicately flowing

Melody Bober

Study Guide

The Entertainer

Scott Joplin, arr. Melody Bober
(pages 46–47)

1-Minute FYI

✔ *The Entertainer,* first published in 1902, is one of Scott Joplin's most popular piano rags. An African-American composer and pianist, Joplin wrote at least 50 rags for piano.

✔ This piece was used in the movie *The Sting,* which was released in 1974. The film was responsible for introducing Joplin's music to many audiences throughout the world.

✔ *The Entertainer* illustrates one of the unique and appealing features of ragtime—the syncopated rhythm of the melody.

5-Minute Warm-Up

These exercises will help you learn the rhythm.

Tap and count aloud each example 3 times a day.

15-Minute Practice Plan

Divide *The Entertainer* into three sections for practice.

Week 1:	Section 1 (measures 1–4)

Week 2:	Section 2 (measures 4–20 and coda)

Week 3:	Section 3 (measures 20–36)

Week 4:	Practice the entire piece.
✔ *Look for patterns that repeat or are similar.*	

 5-Minute Finishing Touches

✔ When performing, avoid playing too fast. In his instruction manual, *School of Ragtime,* Joplin cautioned against playing ragtime too fast.

✔ Always keep the LH quarter notes steady and a little softer than the RH melody.

Study Guide

Study Guide: pages 44–45

The Entertainer

Scott Joplin (1868–1917)
arr. Melody Bober

Section 3

Fiesta Cha-Cha

Melody Bober
(pages 50–55)

1-Minute FYI

✔ *Fiesta Cha-Cha,* a dance for piano duet, will allow you to share music with a friend.

✔ Each section of the piece establishes a different mood, although the tempo doesn't change between sections.

5 Minute Warm-Up

This exercise will help you get a feel for the key of the piece (C Major) as well as help with coordination. Play it 3 times a day.

These exercises will help you with rhythm and coordination.
On your lap, tap and count aloud each example 3 times a day.

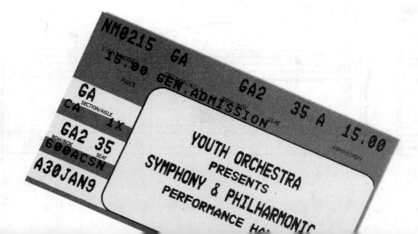

15-Minute Practice Plan (when learning your individual part)

Divide *Fiesta Cha-Cha* into four sections for practice.

Week 1:	Section 1 (measures 1–12)
Week 2:	Section 2 (measures 13–20)
Week 3:	Section 3 (measures 21–29)
Week 4:	Section 4 (measures 30–39)
✔ *Notice that Section 4 is similar to Section 1.*	
Practice the entire piece by section.	

 15-Minute Practice Plan (when practicing with your partner)

Measures 5–12 and 30–35:

Play only the RH of the primo and the LH of the secondo to hear the RH primo melody and the strong LH bass line.

Measures 13–18:

The secondo RH melody should sing out above the other parts. The primo chords should be soft and steady.

Measures 21–29:

Practice playing only the chords (the RH of the secondo and both hands of the primo). Listen that they are played exactly together.

 5-Minute Finishing Touches

✔ Keep a very steady tempo and avoid the tendency to let the piece get faster and faster.

Fiesta Cha-Cha
Secondo

Section 1

Melody Bober

Study Guide: pages 48–49

Fiesta Cha-Cha
Primo

Section 1

Melody Bober

Secondo

Section 3

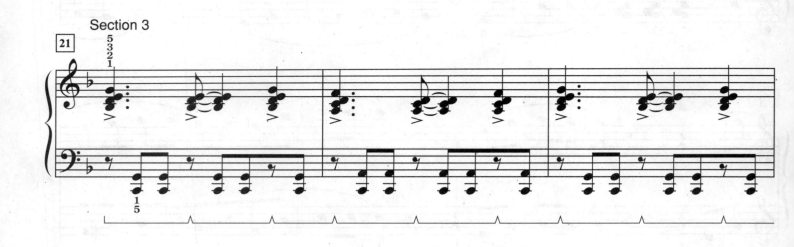

Section 2

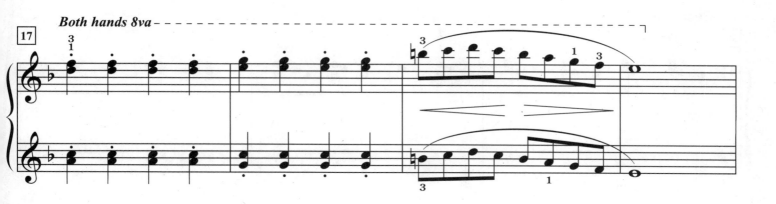

Section 3

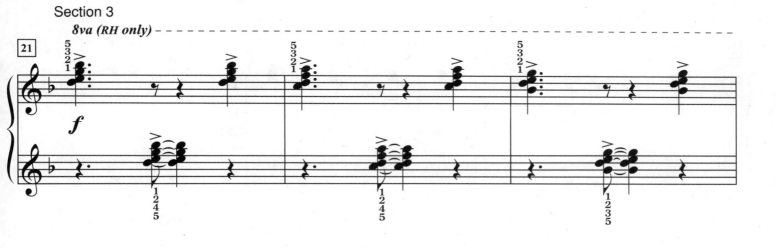

Secondo

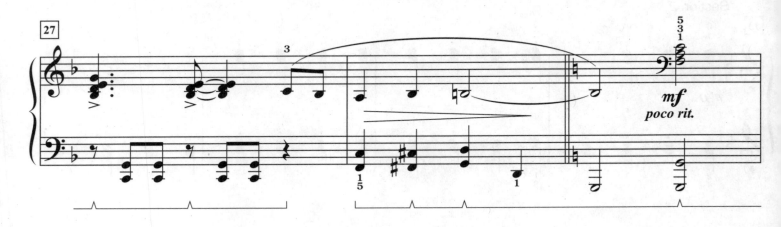

Section 4

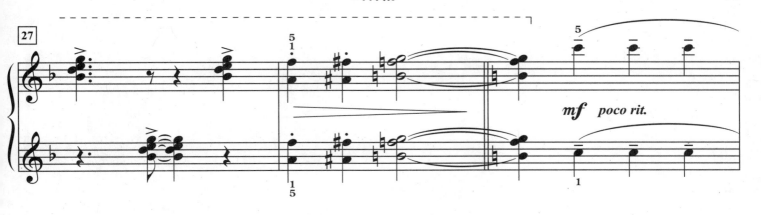

Section 4